HOW THE UNIVERSE
BEGAN

HOW THE UNIVERSE BEGAN

GODS NUMBER 1, 2, AND 3

ROY MANISH

How the Universe Began: Gods Number 1, 2, and 3
Copyright © 2022 Roy Manish

Visit our website at www.StillwaterPress.com for more information.

First Stillwater River Publications Edition

ISBN: 978-1-958217-02-3

12345678910
Written by Roy Manish
Published by Stillwater River Publications,
Pawtucket, RI, USA.

Originally published by Page Publishing, Inc. 2017

Publisher's Cataloging-In-Publication Data
(Prepared by The Donohue Group, Inc.)

Names: Manish, Roy, author.
Title: How the Universe began : Gods Number 1, 2 and 3 / Roy Manish.
Description: First Stillwater River Publications edition. | Pawtucket, RI, USA : Stillwater River Publications, [2022] | Originally published by Page Publishing, Inc. in 2017.
Identifiers: ISBN 9781955123853
    Subjects: LCSH: Creation. | Bible and science. | Myth in the Bible. |
        Bible--Criticism, interpretation, etc. | Mythology.
      Classification: LCC BS651 .M36 2022 | DDC 231.7652--dc23

INTRODUCTION

IN THIS BOOK I am trying to show evidence that the true creator of life is God 1 (the Universe), that we are products of nature through the process of evolution and energy exchange, and that God 2, Yahweh (Jehovah, father of Christ), was a man like us and cloned us in his image.

God 3, Jesus Christ, is the son of God in name only, and was not resurrected from the dead.

HOW THE UNIVERSE BEGAN

GODS NUMBER 1, 2, AND 3

God 1—the Universe
God 2—Yahweh (Jehovah), Father of Christ
God 3—Jesus Christ

GODS NUMBER 1, 2, AND 3

FROM MY CHILDHOOD, I was always a skeptic. A skeptic, in a dictionary's version, is one who doubts the truth of any doctrine or system: one who doubts the existence of God or revelation. But my skepticism urges me on to find the truth of the matter. So in this book, I will try to reveal what I believe is the truth of that age-old mystery, the Bible. It's said a thousand-mile journey starts with the first step, so come with me on an exploration of what is written and my interpretation of the Bible.

The title of my book is *How the Universe Began*, so let's start with Genesis.

VERSE 1—In the beginning, God created the Heaven and the Earth.

VERSE 11—And God said, "Let the Earth bring forth grass, the herb yielding seed and the fruit tree yielding fruit after his kind. Whose seed is in itself, upon the earth.": and it was so.

Let's stop here a minute. At this point, I want to bring out what I believe is one of the keywords in verse 11. It says "Fruit trees yielding fruit after his KIND." Kind is the keyword, meaning "same as," or to put it in another way, God has a fruit tree just like this one he is creating.

VERSE 25—And God made the beast of the earth after his kind.

Here again, we see his creations are after his kind.

VERSE 26—And God said, "Let us make man in our image."

Here again, we have the keywords *let us* and *our image*. OK, let's take (let us).

God is speaking in the plural, so we know

he is not alone. He also says "Let's make man in our image." This tells us he looks like us or we look like them.

Now I would like to get to the meat of my interpretation of what we have going here. Let's take the keywords again "after his kind," "let us," and "our image." Let's start with "after his kind." This tells me that God is copying or duplicating something already in existence somewhere else. Now, getting to "let us," this tells me he is not alone, and the last keywords, "our image," tell me we are talking of human beings just like us.

Here is where I want to show that God, not being here alone on earth, created man in a fashion not unlike what we today are doing with test tube babies and cloning. The only difference was that the whole earth was their test tube.

As we go on into the Bible, I will try to point out the human aspects of God and that they were an advanced civilization from another solar system and were engaged in biological experiments, and we are the results of their experiments. So my theory is that Adam and Eve were test tube babies or clones, which makes us descendants of them. I am also answering the up-to-date question of how to treat a man-made person, which is to use them for replacement parts on slaves. My answer to this is that since the clone is made of the same biological chemistry as us, he would be like us and come under the same laws of nature as us.

Before I move into the Garden of Eden part of my story, I want to condition you more on why I believe God represents an advanced civilization from a solar system far away from us.

Let's assume there is an advanced civilization and they live on a planet like ours. Their quest for knowledge would lead them into exploring space, and at the same time, the other branches of their sciences are being developed as well. They, just like us, would be putting great effort into conquering diseases and ultimately, death.

Now, with conquering death, there would be a drastic change in their civilization and lifestyle. For one thing, their IQ would increase because people could have time to complete all their ideas, which death would rob them of. It would also extend their range of space exploration from one end of the universe to the other; this would also make space theirs.

Now that time and space are no longer a problem, the only thing left to do is explore and experiment on other planets.

Now, if you want to do a biological experiment on something that may cause a problem on your own planet, you have a universe to do it in.

Let's suppose you want to clone a race of people. First, you will find a planet where there will be room for your culture to grow and to mature. Now suppose this planet you find looks like what you want, but it doesn't have everything on it that you need for your clones, such as animal and plant life for food, you will have to bring the animal and plant life from your planet, and being advanced scientifically, you can bring all these life forms in genetic code packaging, which will have thousands of different species and will take up little room on your spaceship.

Now that I have set the format of my theory, let's see how it fits in with the Bible.

UFO group says it is ready for clone age

Medical researchers fear that a Canada-based religious group that says space aliens have instructed it to start cloning humans will ban the technique.

BY AARON ZITNER
Los Angeles Times

VALCOURT, Quebec — In the course of 29 years, Claude Vorilhon held a steady yet information-strewn presence by preaching that who was from another planet created all life on Earth. But in 1998, Vorilhon had unexpectedly legitimate concern to his 5,000 or so followers. The creators are at work to aid their flying saucers and return. It was time to prepare.

And so Vorilhon told their breast to young women in his group to step forward as host cases to the arriving aliens. Members of the Order of the Angels were to devote themselves fully — and in some cases sexually — to the creators and their product on Earth, Vorilhon

According to former members, will devote more than 100 women volunteered.

It is an unusual tale, but the strangest part may be this: today, Vorilhon has won a prominent role in one of the most sober policy decisions before Congress — whether to outlaw human cloning, even as a research tool that might help cure disease.

At the direction of the aliens, Vorilhon says, his group is working to create the world's first cloned child. Some of the Angels have agreed to act as the egg donors and surrogate mothers that the process requires.

Cloning "is the key to eternal life, that's the goal," Vorilhon

see CLONE, D-6

CLAUDE VORILHON, who preaches that scientists from another planet created life on Earth, speaks to visitors to his office at UFOland in Valcourt, Quebec. Vorilhon and his group have become a focal point in the debate over cloning.

FROM THE COVER

creed: Peace, love of science, sexual freed

Clones

Continued from Page D1

—*Cloning has been commonplace in horticulture since ancient times. British researchers achieved the first cloning of an adult mammal in 1996.*

GENESIS CHAPTER 1

VERSE 24—And God said let the earth bring forth the living creature after his kind, cattle and creeping things, and beast of the earth after his kind. And it was so.

GENESIS CHAPTER 2

VERSE 8—And the Lord God planted a garden eastward in Eden and there he put the man whom he had formed.

VERSE 9—And out of the ground made the Lord God to grow every tree that is pleasant to the sight and good for food. The tree of life is also in the midst of the garden and the tree of knowledge of good and evil.

VERSE 12—And the gold of that land is good.

I would like to point out here where God speaks of gold and its quality. A human would be interested in gold.

—Adam and Eve in the act of disobedience.

I can't imagine a god who just created a whole universe giving gold a second thought.

VERSE 16—And the Lord God commanded the man, saying of every tree of the garden, "Thou mayest freely eat."

VERSE 17—"But of the tree of the knowledge of good and evil, thou shalt not eat of it for in the day that thou eatest there of thou shalt surely die."

In verse 17, God is telling Adam not to eat of this tree of knowledge. Here I believe God is testing Adam on his loyalty to him. God also created Eve, and she is also told not to eat from the tree for she would die.

Genesis Chapter 3

VERSE 4—And the serpent said unto the woman, "Ye shall not surely die:"

VERSE 5—"For God doth know that in the day ye eat there of them your eyes shall be opened and ye shall be as Gods, knowing good and evil."

God told Adam and Eve that if they ate of the forbidden tree, they would die. This means they would not die right after eating the fruit, but they would die, rather than live forever.

—Iblis is tempting Eve to eat the fruit.

Iblis is a fallen angel that God had also created but had fallen out of grace with God because he refused to venerate Adam at creation. He and his followers were thrown down from heaven. God called him a beast and a serpent, but he was a man that God had created. Heaven is a spaceship.

GENESIS CHAPTER 3

VERSE 1—Now, Iblis was more subtle than any beast of the field which the Lord God had made, and he said unto the woman, 'Yea, hath God said ye shall not eat of every tree of the garden?"

VERSE 2—And the woman said unto Iblis "We may eat of the fruit of the trees of the garden.

VERSE 3—But of the fruit of the tree which is in the midst of the garden, God hath said, Ye shall not eat of it, neither shall ye touch it, lest ye die."

VERSE 4—And Iblis said unto the woman, "Ye shall not surely die.

VERSE 5—For God doth know that in the day ye eat there of them your eyes shall be opened and ye shall be as Gods knowing good and evil."

Adam and Eve ate of the tree.

VERSE 7—And the eyes of them both were opened, and they knew that they were naked and they sewed fig leaves together and made themselves aprons.

Let's examine this tree of forbidden fruit. If God didn't want Adam and Eve to eat of it, why did he put it there? It would seem to me it was put there to see if Adam and Eve could follow commands or to see if they wished to have knowledge of good and evil, with death being the price of this knowledge.

Iblis knew that Adam and Eve would not die and would become gods themselves. Now, Adam and Eve eat and their eyes are opened.

Now, let's look at the fact that Adam's and Eve's eyes are opened to the fact they know they are naked. What kind of fruit would give you knowledge when you touch or eat it? My theory here would be that God hypnotized Adam and Eve and, under hypnosis, told them of good and evil, but they would not remember it unless they touched or ate of the fruit tree.

To enforce my theory on hypnotism, I will show you later on in my book in the time of Christ where it was used quite often.

GENESIS CHAPTER 3

VERSE 11—And he, (God) said . . . "Who told thee that thou wast naked? Hast thou eaten of the tree? Whereof I commanded thee that thou shouldest not eat?"

Here God asks, 'Who told thee that thou wast naked?" It was when they ate of the fruit that they knew they were naked. This leaves only God, and the only way he could have told them was through hypnosis.

WHO TOLD THEE THAT THOU WAST NAKED ?

VERSE 22—And the Lord God said, "Behold, the man is become as one of us to know good and evil. And now, least he put forth his hand and take also of the tree of life and eat and live forever."

Here, God is saying again that he and man are alike. Also, he is saying that Adam and Eve are not going to die because they ate of the forbidden fruit tree; they are going to die because God is not going to let them eat of the tree of life.

GENESIS CHAPTER 4

VERSE 24—So he drove out man and he placed at the east of the Garden of Eden Cherubims, and a flaming sword which turned every way to keep the way of the tree of life.

Here, you see God chasing Adam from the garden to keep him from the tree of life. Why doesn't God just cut the tree down? Instead, he protects it. Now remember, God said Adam ate of the tree of knowledge and he would live forever if he also ate of the tree of life. Now we see God protecting this tree.

This can only mean God was also eating of this tree of life. It would seem these space people (God) needed an herb or fruit that gave them immortality. When these space people (God) were developing their home planet, they must have found the chemical that stops body cells from degenerating, and they manufactured a plant or tree to produce a fruit with this chemical in it, or maybe the tree is a natural life form on their home planet.

Adam and Eve are evicted from the garden to toil in the earth. Cain and Abel are born. Cain kills Abel. Cain flees from God and finds himself a wife in the land of Nod, and they have a child called Enoch.

It's interesting to note here that Cain interbreeds with an earth woman and conceives a child. Here we have the proof that God didn't start mankind, only reproduced him, for there was already man on earth at the time of creation of Adam and Eve.

Now, Adam has a life span of 930 years before he dies. Remember, he had been eating from the tree of life up until Iblis came along. There is no mention of the time he had spent in the Garden of Eden before his expulsion. My point here is to get the idea across that Adam was building up a reserve of the chemistry of this tree of life, which gave him 930 years of life. The descendants of Adam lived to be over eight hundred years of age, which ran a span of over four thousand years, until Noah was born.

Notice how all the descendants of Adam have inherited his long life span and see what happened when the strain was broken when they intermarried with the people of earth.

GENESIS CHAPTER 6

VERSE 1—And it came to pass when men began to multiply on the face of the Earth, and daughters were born unto them.

VERSE 2—That the sons of God saw the daughters of men [men here means "earth people"], that they were fair and they took them wives of all which they chose.

VERSE 3—And the Lord said, "My spirit shall not always strive with man, for that he also is flesh: yet his days shall be a hundred and twenty years."

Here, in verse 3, God is saying the long life span is going to be diluted when they intermarry with the earth people, whose life span is only one hundred and twenty years.

Verse 4 says there were giants in the earth in those days. Could this mean they (God) were still experimenting to see how big they could make a man grow?

THE END OF THE WORLD

GENESIS CHAPTER 6

VERSE 5—And God saw that the wickedness of man was great in the earth, and that every imagination of the thought of his heart was only evil continually.

VERSE 7—And the Lord said, "I will destroy man, whom I have created. from the face of the earth. Both man and beast, and the creeping things and the fowls of the air, for it repenteth one that I have made them."

VERSE 8—But Noah found grace in the eyes of the Lord.

In verse 7, the Lord says he will destroy all he created. But why does he destroy the animals? Were they wicked also?

Noah builds the ark and brings forth male and female of all animals to the ark. The rains come and flood the earth, destroying all life on it.

This is also the end of man, who was here on earth before Adam and Eve.

(See Genesis 4:16—17 and 6:1—3.)

Noah's ark settles on Mount Ararat after seven months after the rains started. On the twelfth month, the earth was dried of all the floodwaters.

Could they (God) have used some scientific method to cause the earth to flood, such as melting the snow at the poles? Why did it take them so long to get the water back down again? (See Genesis 1:9—10.) God separated water from earth in one day. Why did it take twelve months this time?

Noah and his sons are told to be fruitful and multiply and replenish the earth.

Three hundred and fifty years pass after the flood. The generations of Noah are spreading throughout the land and are building cities.

TOWER OF BABEL

GENESIS CHAPTER 11

VERSE 1—And the whole earth was of one language and of one speech.

VERSE 2—And it came to pass, as they journeyed from the east, that they found a plain in the land of Shinar. And they dwelt there.

VERSE 3—And they said one to another, "Go to, let us make brick and burn them thoroughly." And they had brick for stone, and slime had they for mortar.

VERSE 4—And they said, "Go to, let us build us a city and a tower whose top may reach unto heaven, and let us make us a name, lest we be scattered abroad upon the face of the whole earth."

VERSE 5—<u>And the Lord came down</u> to see the city and the tower which the children of men built.

VERSE 6—And the Lord said, "Behold, the people are one and they have all one language, and this they begin to do. And now nothing will be restrained from them which they have imagined to do."

Let's look at this situation. The people settle in the plains and want to build a city and a tower. But God doesn't want this. Why not? Other people build cities. It must be the tower, for they are building it in fear of being scattered around the earth. God says nothing will stop the people from what they want to do.

What do they want to do with this tower? And why is God so against it? Could it be that if the people built this tower, they could see farther and might see a rocket ship at a launch site?

VERSE 7—"Go to. <u>Let us go down,</u> and there confound their language, that they may not understand one another's speech." And the Lord scattered them around the earth.

How was this done? Rocket ship or some type of aircraft?

Remember, God must be close by in order to keep tabs on these people he is watching, but keep in mind he shows himself only. His men and equipment are out of sight.

Here is another example. At this time in Genesis, you begin to see angels. Could angels be another name for the crew of his rocket ship?

Let's read Genesis 18:1 and see if they fit the description of mortal man.

GENESIS CHAPTER 18

VERSE 1—And the Lord appeared unto him in the plains of Man, and he sat in the tent door in the heat of the day.

VERSE 2—And he lifted up his eyes and looked and lo, three men stood by him, and when he saw them he ran to meet them from the tent door and bowed himself toward the ground.

VERSE 3—And said, "My Lord, if now to have found favor in thy sight pass not away, I pray thee, from thy servant.

VERSE 4—Let a little water, I pray you, be fetched, and wash your feet and rest yourselves under the tree.

VERSE 5—And I will fetch a morsel of bread and comfort ye your hearts. After that ye shall pass on, for therefore are ye come to your servant." And they said, "Do as thou hast said."

Genesis Chapter 19: Angels Visit Lot and Deliver Him from Sodom

VERSE 13—Angels are speaking to Lot. "For we will destroy this place because the cry of them is waxen great before the face of the Lord, and the Lord hath sent us to destroy it."

VERSE 24—Then, the Lord rained upon Sodom, and rained upon Gomorra brimstone and fire from the Lord out of heaven.

VERSE 26—But his wife looked back from behind him and she became a pillar of salt.

Angels tell Lot to leave Sodom for they are going to destroy it. How are they going to destroy it? Are they going to drop a bomb on it?

Today, Sodom and Gomorrah have been found, and evidence proves that these two cities did exist; they also found that the cities were built over oil and sulfur deposits. Could they have dropped a bomb, which could have ignited those oil deposits?

Why was Lot's wife turned into a pillar of salt when she looked back at the destruction of Sodom? Did they destroy her because she might have been a witness to an aircraft dropping a bomb?

Why would they not want her to see an aircraft? Could it be they didn't want man to come to understand what technology could do?

EXODUS

GOD TELLS MOSES to free his people from the bondage of the Egyptians and tell the Pharaoh of God's message.

EXODUS 4

VERSE 1—And Moses answered and said, "But behold, they will not believe me, nor hearken unto my voice: for they will say, 'The Lord hath not appeared unto thee.'"

Moses has a good point here. Why doesn't the Lord see the Pharaoh himself? Is it because he is trying to keep an illusion of a spiritual God, or is he playing it safe, not putting his life in danger in the Pharaoh's land? Even if he is immortal, a spear in his back could kill him.

VERSE 2—And the Lord said unto him, "What is that in thine hand?" And he said, "A rod."

VERSE 3—And he said, "Cast it on the ground." And he cast it on the ground, and it became a serpent: and Moses fled from before it.

VERSE 4—And the Lord said unto Moses, "Put forth thine hand and take it by the tail." And he put forth his hand and caught it and it became a rod in his hand.

I believe what happened here was that the rod was always a rod, but a mental image was transmitted to Moses that made the rod appear to be a serpent. And I believe that most of the events that went on in the Pharaohs land, such as frogs and insects, were tricks of a magician.

Remember, the Pharaoh had magicians also. But God, being more intelligent, had the better tricks.

The dictionary says this about *magic*:
"the pretended art of working by the powers
or assistance of supernatural beings."

THE LORD LEADS THEM
OUT OF EGYPT

EXODUS 13

VERSE 21—And the Lord went before them by day in a pillar of a cloud to lead them the way and by night in a pillar of fire to give them light to go by day and night.

VERSE 22—He took not away the pillar of the cloud by day, nor the pillar of fire by night from before the people.

ISRAELITES CROSS
THE RED SEA

EXODUS 14

VERSE 19—And the angel of God which went before the camp of Israel removed. And went behind them, and the pillar of the cloud went from before their face and stood behind them.

VERSE 20—And it came between the camp of the Egyptians and the camp of Israel and it was a cloud and darkness to them, but it gave light by night to these so that the one came not near the other all the night.

Here again, I believe it was some sort of smoke screen device, maybe something like our moon lander, and at night the fire would become visible.

THE RED SEA OPENS

VERSE 21—And Moses stretched out his hand over the sea: and the Lord caused the sea to go back by a strong east wind all that night and made the sea dry land. The waters were divided.

VERSE 22—And the children of Israel went into the midst of the sea upon the dry ground and the waters were a wall unto them on their right hand and on their left.

VERSE 23—And the Egyptians pursued and went in after them to the midst of the sea, even all Pharaoh's horses, his chariots, and his horsemen.

VERSE 24—And it came to pass, that in the morning watch, the Lord looked unto the host of the Egyptians through the pillar of fire and of the cloud and troubled the host of the Egyptians.

VERSE 25—And took off their chariot wheels that they drove them heavily: so that the Egyptians said, let us flee from the face of Israel: for the Lord fighteth for them against the Egyptians.

VERSE 26—And the Lord said unto Moses, "Stretch out thine hand over the sea, that the waters may come again upon the Egyptians, upon their chariots and upon their horsemen."

VERSE 27—And Moses stretched forth his hand over the sea and the sea returned to his strength when the morning appeared and the Egyptians fled against it and the Lord overthrew the Egyptians in the midst of the sea.

VERSE 28—And the water returned and covered the chariots and the horsemen, and all the host of Pharaoh that come into the sea after them. There remained not so much as one of them.

CHAPTER 15

VERSE 8—And with the blast of thy nostrils the waters were gathered together, the floods stood upright as a heap, and the depths were congealed in the heart of the sea.

Let's examine the possible ways of getting six hundred thousand people across the sea. First, you could consider a boat, but a boat would be tremendous in size, and where would you keep it? Keeping in mind you are supposed to be a supernatural force, so for this reason also, you can't use a boat. This also rules out a bridge. A supernatural force would not build a bridge either.

You would want something you can keep out of sight until you're ready to use it. So here is what I believe they did. They (God and his angels) found the narrowest point of the Red Sea, which is closest to Mount Sinai, and built two dams across the Red Sea, parallel to each other, and let's say for the sake of argument twenty feet across and whatever the depth of the water. We would keep them just at the water level so that wouldn't be seen from the shore and the water could flow across them.

Remember, we are in the wilderness, so we can construct them unnoticed, and they more than likely built them out of wood for it's only a temporary structure. Now that the dams are built, we could go ahead with the exodus of the Israelites.

I will go step by step on each verse, starting with verse 19 of Exodus 14, and explain what I think happened here.

VERSE 19—And the Angel of God which went before the camp of Israel removed and went behind them.

The Angel of God here, I believe, is a machine, something like our moon lander, which has hovering capability.

VERSE 20—And it came between the camp of the Egyptians and the camp of the Israelites and it was a cloud and darkness to them but it gave light by night to these so that the one came not near the other all the night.

We now have both camps at the shore of the Red Sea, separated by a machine blowing smoke. Notice the time. It was daylight when they first were separated and going into the night.

VERSE 21—And Moses stretched out his hand over the sea and the Lord caused the sea to go back by a strong east wind all that night and made the sea dry land.

Here, I believe Moses's outstretched hand is a signal to God's angels on the other side of the sea to start up pumps, which were pumping water out from between the two dams. The strong east winds could be caused by a giant fan, which would be used to cool this massive water pump and at the same time

keep the smoke blowing at the Egyptians.
Remember, they were camped all night.

IT'S MORNING NOW

VERSE 22—And the children of Israel went into the midst of the sea upon the dry ground and the waters were a wall unto them on their right hand and on their left.

Here, the water is gone, and the ground is dry.

VERSE 23—And the Egyptians pursued and went in after them to the midst of the sea.

VERSE 24—And it came to pass that in the morning watch the Lord looked unto the host of the Egyptians through the pillar of fire and of the cloud and troubled the host of the Egyptians.

VERSE 25—And took off their chariots' wheels that they drove them heavily so that the Egyptians said let us flee from the face of Israel for the Lord fighteth for them against the Egyptians.

Here, it says God took the wheels off their chariots; he apparently had to slow them down. I get the impression the Egyptians were breaking through the smoke screen, and how was he removing the wheels from the chariots? How about a laser beam?

VERSE 26—And the Lord said unto Moses, "Stretch out thine hand over the sea that the waters may come again upon the Egyptians."

VERSE 27—And Moses stretched forth his hand over the sea and the sea returned.

VERSE 28—And the water returned and covered the chariots and the horsemen and all the host of Pharaoh that come into the sea after them, there remained not so much as one of them.

CHAPTER 15

VERSE 8—*Moses is speaking to God:* And with a blast of thy nostrils the waters were gathered together, the floods stood upright as a heap and the depth were congealed in the heart of the sea.

Here, I think the "blast of thy nostrils" was a rocket pulling up stakes that held the dams together, and "the depth were congealed" means they froze the mud of the sea floor, which was described as being dry.

With the technology they had, this could have been done. Remember, God also designed Noah's ark, which was seaworthy for more than seven months without a trial run.

Centuries-Old Writings Show UFOs Visited Earth in 4,000 B.C.

By BOB TEMMEY

Centuries-old writings in Sanskrit, the classical language of India and Hinduism, prove that aliens from outer space visited earth, insists a renowned scholar.

Fifty years of researching these ancient works convinces me that there are living beings on other planets, and that they visited earth as far back as 4,000 B.C., says Dr. V. Raghavan, retired head of the Sanskrit department of India's prestigious University of Madras.

"There's just a mass of fascinating information about flying machines, even fantastic science fiction weapons, that can be found in the translations of the Vedas (scriptures), Indian epics and other ancient Sanskrit texts.

"In the Mahabharata (writings) there is a demon of diving lightning and rays, weapons, even a kind of hypnotic weapon.

"And in the Ramayana (writings) there is a description of Vimanas, or flying machines, that navigated at great heights with the aid of quicksilver and a great propulsive wind.

"These were space vehicles similar to the so-called flying saucers reported throughout the world today.

"The Ramayana even describes a two-storied aerial chariot with windows and a wonderful divine car that sped through the air.

"In another passage, there is mention of a chariot being seen sailing overhead like a moon.

"The references in the Mahabharata are to its air-touring. At Rama's behest ...

the magnificent chariot rose up to a mountain of cloud with a tremendous din. And later it "was like a glow in the sky ... in summer ... which was as brilliant as the sun and made a noise like the thunder of a storm."

From the ancient Vymanika Shastra (Science of Aeronautics) comes this description of a Vimana: "An apparatus which can go by its own force, from place to place or globe to globe."

Said Dr. Raghavan: "The Vymanika Shastra devotes verse with minute detailing. There's one ...

... parts — of which the machine consists — are described, including a photographing mirror underneath. The text also mentions kinds of metal that are needed to construct the flying vehicle. Metals suitable, light and heat-absorbing are of 16 kinds.

"But only three of them are known to us today. The rest remain untranslatable."

One top expert who agrees with Dr. Raghavan's interpretations is Dr. A.V. Krishna

Murty, professor of aeronautics at the Indian Institute of Science in Bangalore.

"It is true," he says, "that the ancient Indian Vedas and other texts refer to aeronautics, spaceships, flying machines and even astronauts.

"A study of the Sanskrit texts has convinced me that ancient India did know the secret of building flying machines — and that those machines were patterned after spaceships coming from other planets."

This map shows where the Israelites crossed the Red Sea, which is now called the Gulf of Suez. The distance of the Red Sea that they crossed was a little over a mile.

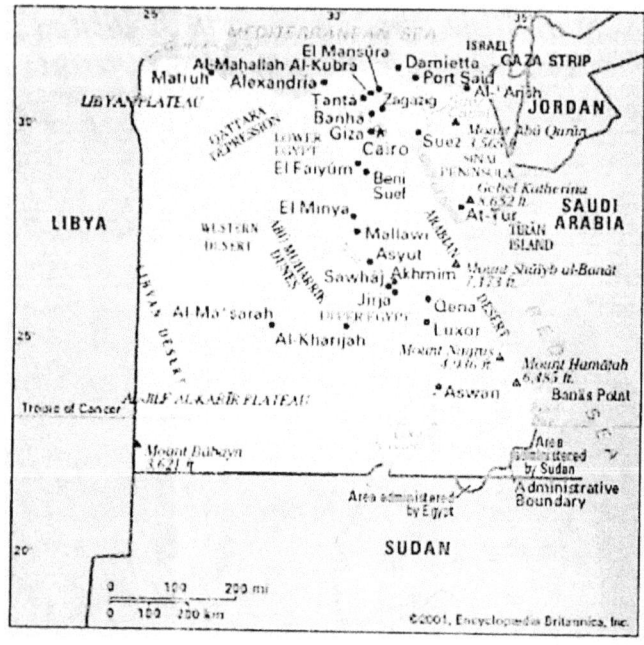

Keep in mind as you read that I am trying to point out that God and his angels are only men just like us. And notice that God and his angels show themselves to only a select few.

If anyone other than the chosen ones see God, they will be killed. For an example, see what God says in Exodus 19:12: "And thou shalt set bounds unto the people round about, saying, 'Take heed to yourselves, they ye go not up into the mount, or touch the border of it. Who so ever toucheth the mount shall be surely put to death.'"

—A rocket lands on Mount Sinai?

MOUNT SINAI

VERSE 18—And Mount Sinai was altogether on a smoke, because the Lord descended upon it in fire and the smoke thereof ascended as the smoke of a furnace and the whole mount quaked greatly.

God speaks to Moses through a PA system?

VERSE 19—And when the voice of the trumpet sounded long and waxed louder and louder, Moses spake, and God answered him by a voice.

EXODUS CHAPTER 20

VERSE 2—"I am the Lord thy God, which have brought thee out of the land of Egypt, out of the house of bondage.

VERSE 3—Thou shalt have no other Gods before me."

Let's examine Exodus 20:2—3. God doesn't recognize the Egyptians as his people. As we have been going along in the Bible from Noah on, these are all God's people, but why is God out of touch with the Egyptians, and why do the Egyptians believe in another God? Could the Egyptians be a race from another God?

Let's look at verse 3 again: "Thou shalt have no other Gods before me." What other gods is he referring to?

VERSE 4—"Thou shalt not make unto thee any graven image or any likeness of anything that is in heaven above or that is in the earth beneath, or that is in the water under the earth."

At this point, I would like to interject this one statement. At the present time, UFOs are reported to be seen coming out of the waters. Could UFOs have been around at this time in the Bible? Let's move on to verse 5.

VERSE 5—"Thou shalt not bow down thyself to them nor serve them: for I the Lord thy God am a jealous God, evicting the iniquity of the fathers upon the children unto the third and fourth generation of them that hate me."

EXODUS CHAPTER 23

VERSE 13—"And in all things that I have said unto you be circumspect: (cautious) and make no mention of the name of other gods. Neither let it be heard out of thy mouth."

Around the world today, there is evidence that ancient races of people had met gods and had made idols of their existence. Also, these ancient people had knowledge of things of which we are just coming to understand today.

Could these be the gods that God was referring to? If they were just pagan gods, why was he jealous? Could there have been a power struggle between God and other gods that also come to earth? Why did God have a problem finding land for his people?

If there were other Gods, it will not be found in the Bible, as God said in Exodus 23:13, "And make no mention of the name of other gods. Neither let it be heard out of thy mouth."

THE TABERNACLE

THE TABERNACLE IS BUILT by God's direction and, by its design, is a large static generator, which is intended to keep the unappointed away. To touch it, you would be electrocuted; it is also a two-way radio station in which God and Moses are in communication. It is also a place where God receives a feast, which is cooked to his liking and done in a direction from which he could watch it being prepared.

LEVITICUS

CHAPTER 1

VERSE 1—And the Lord called unto Moses and spake unto him out of the tabernacle of the congregation saying—

VERSE 2—"Speak unto the children of Israel, and say unto them, 'If any man of you bring an offering unto the Lord, ye shall bring your offering of the cattle even of the herd and of the flock.'

VERSE 11—And he shall kill it on the side of the altar NORTHWARD before the Lord."

Here, again, I would like to point out, as I said in the "Tower of Babel," that God was in the distance, watching them building the tower; and here he says to kill the offerings on the north side so he can watch. So this tells me God has a base camp always near by the Israelites so he can watch them.

ELECTROCUTION

SECOND BOOK OF SAMUEL, CHAPTER 6

VERSE 6—And when they came to Nachon's threshing floor, Uzzah put forth his hand to the ark of God, and took hold of it, for the oxen shook it.

VERSE 7—And the anger of the Lord was kindled against Uzzah and God smote him there for his error and there he died by the Ark of God.

SUMMARY OF GOD 2

A T THE START of this book, I began with God 1, and said God created heaven and earth, as the Bible states, and that this was done in six days. I don't believe this to be true.

In Genesis 1:2, it says, "And the earth was without form and void." This means there was no earth.

VERSE 3—And God said, "Let there be light." And there was light.

VERSE 4—And God saw the light, that it was good and God divided the light from the darkness.

Here, it says God divided the light from the dark. Light and dark are not separate; dark is the absence of light.

VERSE 5—And God called the light day, and the darkness he called night, and the evening and the morning were the first day.

In order to have a morning and evening, you need a sunrise and a sunset, but you need a planet for the sun to rise and set on, and there is no Earth yet.

VERSE 6—And God said, "Let there be a firmament [sky] in the midst of the waters and let it divide the waters from the waters."

VERSE 7—And God made the firmament [sky] and divided the waters, which were under the firmament [sky] from the waters which were above the firmament [sky] and it was so.

VERSE 8—And God called the firmament [sky] heaven. And the evening and the morning were the second day.

So far, we have sky in the midst (center) of water.

VERSE 9—And God said, "Let the waters under the heaven [sky] be gathered

together unto one place, and let the dry
land appear." And it was so.

Where did the dry land come from?

VERSE 10—And God called the dry land
earth: and the gathering together of the
waters called the seas. And God saw that
it was good.

I feel that someone who just created the universe would have a better explanation of the
creation of the earth than just putting a sky
in the middle of water.

But if you just created a man, and you
tell him that you are God, the man would
probably want to know where the earth
came from, so you would have to tell him
something; and since you just created him,
why not tell him you made the universe too?
Keep in mind, I believe that we are clones,
and I also believe that UFOs and God are
connected, or to put it another way, they are
one and the same.

In God 2, 1 was stating they were in rockets, but add six thousand years of technology to them, which brings us up to now. I think a UFO fits the kind of aircraft they would have. Just look at the technology we have developed in less than a hundred years: radio, television, cars, rockets, jets, laser beams, computers, robots, atomic generators and subs, satellites, man landing on the moon, probes traveling through space sending back pictures of planets millions of miles away, cures of diseases, organ transplants, test tube babies and cloning—and this is just to name a few.

We are now just starting to get into the spiritual nature of man with ESP, out-of-the-body experiments, reincarnation, and life in another dimension, with all this being done in such a short span of time. I find it very acceptable for a race of people who came here in rockets thousands of years ago to be flying in aircraft as we describe as UFOs today.

I believe the earth, moon, stars, and other planets came into existence on their own through the big bang theory.

I also believe man evolved through evolution from the monkey and was in the upward swing toward what we are today, but science says there is a missing link between prehistoric man and us.

I feel the link isn't missing; it is just the end of that chain. For when God ended the world, he also ended the evolutionary chain of man, which would have led prehistoric man to us.

When God created Adam and Eve, he jumped time in the evolution of man, for he created man whose design was further down the chain of evolution, which shows up as though there was a link missing.

As I interpret the Bible, God came to earth with others and set up a base camp. Not to confuse the issue more, let me put it this way: a much more advanced group of people came to earth and found earth in its early state of man's development and, for whatever reason, created man after themselves. I would think to speed up the mental growth of man, but it must have gone sour, so they destroyed the earth and all things on it except for Noah and his family and tried again, which brings us to where we are today.

The best way I can explain the situation for those days in the Bible is to say a zookeeper takes care of the animals, but doesn't live with them. Just as in the Bible, the advanced men didn't live with the people; they were always in the distance.

And if we have an advanced civilization living somewhere else, what kind of evidence of their existence would there be?

I feel the evidence is the pyramids, Atlantis, Stonehenge, Easter Island, and all the other places that indicate creations of which man was incapable of doing. And why were they created? Could it be they wanted man to awaken to the fact that they were also just men, the gods that came to earth and created us? I think so.

I also feel they are still here today and we know them as UFOs.

GOD 3

JESUS CHRIST

I MUST POINT OUT here that God has been here for a few years and their technology has also been increasing.

Here in "God 3," I will try to point out some of the progress they have made.

THE BIRTH OF CHRIST

SAINT LUKE

CHAPTER 1

VERSE 26—And in the sixth month the angel Gabriel was sent from God unto a city of Galilee, named Nazareth.

VERSE 27—To a virgin espoused to a man whose name was Joseph of the house of David, and the virgin's name was Mary.

VERSE 28—And the angel came unto her, and said, "Hail. Thou that art highly favored, the Lord is with thee: blessed art thou among women."

VERSE 29—And when she saw him she was troubled at his saying: and cast in her mind what manner of salutation this should be.

VERSE 30—And the angel said unto her, "Fear not, Mary for thou hast found favor with God.

VERSE 31—And behold, thou shalt conceive in thy womb and bring forth a son and shalt call him Jesus.

VERSE 32—He shall be great and shall be called the son of the highest: and the

Lord God shall give unto him the throne of his father David.

VERSE 33—And he shall reign over the house of Jacob forever and of his kingdom there shall be no end."

VERSE 34—Then said Mary unto the angel. "How shall this be, seeing I know not a man?"

VERSE 35—And the angel answered and said unto her. "The Holy Ghost shall come upon thee, and the power of the Highest shall overshadow thee: there-fore also that holy thing which shall be born of thee shall be called the Son of God."

ROMANS CHAPTER 1

VERSE 3—Concerning his son Jesus Christ our Lord which was made of the seed of David according to the flesh.

VERSE 4—And declared to be the Son of God with power according to the spirit of holiness by the resurrection from the dead.

Also in Romans it tells us the father of Jesus was David. David was dead years before Jesus was conceived. God saved the sperm of David. My interpretation here is that Mary was artificially inseminated while under hypnosis, and I believe the Holy Ghost, or Holy Spirit, is really the laws of nature, which God and his angels have mastered. I see the Bible as a time clock, cleverly written so not to tell you too much but putting in enough clues so that when we reach a certain level of technology, it will unravel its secrets.

Let's get back to Mary.

SAINT MATTHEW CHAPTER 1

VERSE 18—Now the birth of Jesus Christ was on this wise. When, as his mother, Mary was espoused to Joseph, before they came together, she was found with child of the Holy Ghost.

VERSE 19—Then Joseph her husband, being a just man and not willing to make her a public example, was minded to put her away privately.

VERSE 20—But while he thought on these things, behold the angel of the Lord appeared unto him in a dream saying, "Joseph, thou son of David, fear not to take unto thee Mary thy wife: for that which is conceived in her is of the Holy Ghost.

VERSE 21—And she shall bring forth a son and thou shalt call his name Jesus, for he shall save his people from their sins."

In verse 20, it's saying an angel appeared in a dream. I don't think it was a dream. I would suspect a thought transmission was made to him. I believe God had the means to do such a feat. We are coming into the age of telepathy now. I think God was proficient at it.

VERSE 22—Now all this was done, that it might be fulfilled which was spoken of the Lord by the prophet, saying—

VERSE 23—"Behold, a virgin shall be with child and shall bring forth a son, and they shall call his name Emmanuel which being interpreted, is God with us."

VERSE 24—Then Joseph, being raised from sleep, did as the angel of the Lord had bidden him, and took unto him his wife.

Here, in verse 24, I see Joseph being wakened from a hypnotic state of which he was told what to do concerning the marriage of Mary.

As we look at what went on in the time of Christ where prophets are concerned, you will see that they had no psychic ability but were told what to say under hypnosis. For an example, let's look at Saint Luke.

SAINT LUKE CHAPTER 1

VERSE 19—And the angel answering said unto him, "I am Gabriel, that stand in the presence of God: and sent to speak unto thee, aid to show thee these glad tidings.

VERSE 20—And, behold, thou shall be dumb and not able to speak, until the day that these things shall be performed, because thou believest not my words which shall be fulfilled in their season."

Jesus is born in Bethlehem.

SAINT MATTHEW CHAPTER 2

VERSE 7—Then Herod, when he had privily called the wise men, inquired of them diligently what time the star appeared.

VERSE 8—And he sent them to Bethlehem, and said, "Go and search diligently for the young child and when ye have found him, bring me word again, that I may come and worship him also."

VERSE 9—When they had heard the King, they departed and lo, the star which they saw in the east went before them till it came and stood over where the young child was.

The star here has to be some sort of aircraft, for if a star were to move as described here, the neighboring planets would leave their orbits and collide with other solar systems, causing a disrupting of great magnitude.

VERSE 10—When they saw the star they rejoiced with exceeding great joy.

VERSE 11—And when they were come into the house they saw the young child with Mary, his mother, and fell down and worshipped him. And when they had opened their treasures they presented unto him gifts: gold, frankincense and myrrh.

VERSE 12—And being warned of God in a dream that they should not return to Herod, they departed into their own country another way.

VERSE 13—And when they were departed behold, the angel of the Lord appeared to Joseph in a dream saying, "Arise and take the young child and his mother and flee into Egypt and be thou there until I bring thee word, for Herod will seek the young child to destroy him."

VERSE 14—When he arose, he took the young child and his mother by night and departed into Egypt.

VERSE 15—And was there until the death of Herod: that it might be fulfilled which was spoken of the Lord by the prophet, saying out of Egypt have I called my son.

VERSE 16—Then Herod, when he saw that he was mocked of the wise men was exceeding wroth, and sent forth and slew all the children that were in Bethlehem and in all the coasts thereof from two years old and under, according to the time which he had diligently inquired of the wise men.

VERSE 17—Then was fulfilled that which was spoken by Jeremy the prophet, saying—

VERSE 18—"In Rama was there a voice heard; lamentation and weeping and great mourning. Rachel weeping for her children and would not be comforted, because they are not."

VERSE 19—But when Herod was dead, behold an angel of the Lord appeareth in a dream to Joseph in Egypt.

VERSE 20—Saying, "Arise and take the young child and his mother and go into the land of Israel, for they are dead which sought the young child's life."

VERSE 21—And he arose and took the young child and his mother and came into the Land of Israel.

VERSE 22—But when he heard that Archelaus did reign in Judaea in the room of his father Herod, he was afraid to go thither: not withstanding being warned of God in a dream, he turned aside into the parts of Galilee.

VERSE 23—And he came and dwelt in a city called Nazareth: that it might be fulfilled which was spoken by the prophets, he shall be called a Nazarene.

In verse 13, Joseph is told in a dream to flee into Egypt, for Herod would destroy the child. God has the power to change man's mind, but why does he let Herod slay all the children in Bethlehem? Was it just to have his prophecies come true, as in verses 17 and 18, which tell of the prophets saying it was fulfilled that the children would be slain?

When God released the Israelites from the Pharaoh in Egypt, he said, "I will harden his heart," and made him pursue them so he could slay the Egyptians in the Red Sea, so we know he had the ability to change men's minds, yet he allowed all those children to be killed. Was this done to make a dramatic entrance of Jesus into the world, so that people would be impressed at the worth of Christ?

SAINT MATTHEW CHAPTER 4

VERSE 1—The temptation of Christ. Then was Jesus led up of the spirit into the wilderness to be tempted of the devil.

First off, let me say I believe the devil is a member of God's team, which plays the negative role for testing and demonstration purposes. Verse 1 says Jesus was led up of the spirit into the wilderness to be tempted of the devil. Who led Jesus? I suspect God led him. It also says "led up of the spirit," which means he was on a mental trip into the wilderness, so keep in mind that Jesus is not physically being tempted; it is mental.

VERSE 2—And when he had fasted forty days and forty nights he was afterward and hungered.

Let me try to set the situation here again. I have to assume he is in a reclined position under controlled conditions in which he is in an out-of-body experience in which he is fed information, of which you are about to read next in verse 3.

VERSE 3—And when the tempter came to him he said, "If thou be the Son of God, command that these stones be made bread."

VERSE 4—But he answered and said, "It is written man shall not live by bread alone, but by every word that proceedeth out of the mouth of God."

VERSE 5—Then the devil taketh him up into the Holy City, and setteth him on a pinnacle of the temple.

VERSE 6—And saith unto him, "If thou be the Son of God cast thyself down, for it is written He shall give his angels charge concerning thee and in their hands they shall bear thee up, lest at any time thou dash thy foot against a stone."

VERSE 7—Jesus said unto him, "It is written again thou shalt not tempt the Lord thy God."

VERSE 8—Again, the devil taketh him up into an exceeding high mountain and sees with him all the kingdoms of the world and the glory of them.

VERSE 9—And saith unto him, "All these things will I give thee, if thou wilt fall down and worship me."

Here, in verse 9, you see the same doctrine as God's, that if you worship him, he will make you rich. See 1 Chronicles 29:25.

> And the Lord magnified Solomon exceedingly in the sight of all Israel and bestowed upon him such royal majesty as had not been on any king before him in Israel.

VERSE 10—Then saith Jesus unto him, "Get thee hence Satan. For it is written; thou shalt worship the Lord thy God and him only shalt thou serve."

VERSE 11—Then the devil leaveth him and behold, angels came and ministered unto him.

Notice how the devil leaves without so much as a threat. He doesn't say to Jesus "Obey me or else."

VERSE 17—From that time Jesus began to preach and to say, "Repent: for the kingdom of heaven is at hand."

I believe when Jesus says "the kingdom of heaven is at hand," he is saying that God has made a technological breakthrough to where they are in control of the energy side of the universe, or to put it another way, they are interdimensional and can use and control this dimension of which we live and also the dimension in which we go to when we die.

All we have read on UFOs today, about how they appear as lights hovering in the sky and disappear before our eyes and their antigravity method of propulsion, all fit in this portion of the Bible.

SAINT MATTHEW, CHAPTER 15

VERSE 24—But the ship was now in the midst of the sea, tossed with waves, for the wind was contrary.

VERSE 25—And in the fourth watch of the night Jesus went unto them, walking on the sea.

VERSE 26—And when the disciples saw him walking on the sea they were troubled saying, it is a spirit, and they cried out for fear.

VERSE 27—But straightway Jesus spake unto them saying, "Be of good cheer, it is I, be not afraid."

VERSE 28—And Peter answered him and said "Lord, if it be thou bid me come unto thee on the water."

VERSE 29—And he said come, and when Peter was come down out of the ship, he walked on the water to go to Jesus.

VERSE 30—But when he saw the wind boisterous he was afraid and beginning to sink he cried saying: "Lord save me."

VERSE 31—And immediately Jesus stretched forth his hand and caught him and said unto him: "O thou of little faith wherefore didst thou doubt?"

VERSE 32—And when they were come into the ship the wind ceased.

Here, we have Jesus walking on the water, and it is night. What I envision here is a UFO hovering over Jesus, canceling out gravity, which is allowing him to be weightless. Peter walks on the water also, but sinks shortly. I believe he sank in the water because they wanted him to sink, and why is the wind violent? It doesn't say anything about the sea being rough, but I believe it must have been if the wind was violent. This tells me whatever the force was that was keeping Jesus on top of the water was also affecting the sea.

Verse 32 says the wind became calm when they entered the ship. This tells me that the violent winds were manufactured as a side effect of the antigravity force on the sea, and when Jesus was aboard the ship, this force was turned off.

Let me add here that it has been reported that a UFO lifted a car with its passengers in it and moved it 4,100 miles without incident.

CHAPTER 17

VERSE 1—And after six days Jesus taketh Peter, James and John his brother, and bringeth them up into a high mountain apart.

VERSE 2—And was transfigured before them and his face did shine as the sun and his raiment was white as the light.

VERSE 3—And behold there appeared unto them Moses and Elias talking with him.

VERSE 4—Then answered Peter and said unto Jesus, "Lord it is good for us to be here if thou will let us make here three tabernacles, one for thee and one for Moses and one for Elias."

VERSE 5—While he yet spake, behold a bright cloud overshadowed them and behold a voice out of the cloud which said: "This is my beloved Son in whom I am well pleased, hear ye him."

VERSE 6—And when the disciples heard it they fell on their face and were sore afraid.

VERSE 7—And Jesus came and touched them and said, "Arise and be not afraid."

Here, again, I would point out in verse 5, "a bright cloud overshadowed them," which fits a description of a UFO, and God speaks to them from this cloud. As you have read in "God 2," we saw God appearing in a cloud of smoke, fire, and thunder, which I said was a rocket, but remember, God has been here on earth for some six thousand years or more;

and more than likely, he has been back and forth to his own planet, where technology has been growing and using this technology here on earth. So for this reason, I believe they are not now using rockets anymore.

VERSE 8—And when they had lifted up their eyes they saw no man, save Jesus only.

VERSE 9—And as they came down from the mountain, Jesus charged them, saying "Tell the vision to no man until the Son of man be risen again from the dead."

VERSE 10—And his disciples asked him, saying, "Why then say the scribes that Elias must first come?"

VERSE 11—And Jesus answered and said unto them, "Elias truly shall first come, and restore all things.

VERSE 12—But I say unto you, that Elias is come already and they knew him not, but have done unto him whatsoever they listed, likewise shall also the Son of man suffer of them."

VERSE 13—Then the disciples understood that he spake unto them of John the Baptist.

Moses and Elias appear on the mountain with Jesus. They appear in the spirit for they are both dead. Elias is John the Baptist. He is also going to come to restore all things, which will be at the time Jesus is crucified.

You can see here that they are very capable of handling the energy of life in the other dimension that I believe we all go to after death.

(See "Life After Death" in "God 1.")

Also notice Jesus's death has already been planned.

Here, in Matthew 20:18, Jesus tells of how he will die.

VERSE 18—"Behold we go up to Jerusalem and the son of man shall be betrayed unto the chief priests and unto the scribes, and they shall condemn him to death.

VERSE 19—And shall deliver him to the Gentiles to mock and to scourge and to crucify him, and the third day he shall rise again."

Were all the roles of the people who had a part in the crucifixion of Jesus coincidental, or were all these people somehow programmed to fulfill his prognostication?

This is to say, if Jesus could see into the future of the events that led to his death, then this means that all people are controlled by a force that determines their destiny, and we have no freedom of choice; and if this is so, then the force that controls our destiny should have been altered and all sinners could be changed to righteous people.

Since God made no mention of a force of destiny that controls minds of men and was dealing with the people themselves, I have to assume that the people that were involved with his death were programmed to fulfill what God wanted for Jesus's destiny.

JESUS CRUCIFIED

SAINT MATTHEW CHAPTER 27

VERSE 46—And about the ninth hour Jesus cried with a loud voice saying "Eli, Eli, lama sabachthani?" That is to say, My God, My God, why hast thou forsaken me?

In this verse, I interpret that Jesus has lost faith that God would restore his life and has fear of impending death.

Let's go back to Matthew 26:38. Here Jesus says, "My soul is exceeding sorrowful, even unto death, tarry ye here and watch with me."

VERSE 39—"O my father, if it be possible, let this cup pass from me: nevertheless not as I will, but as thou wilt.

VERSE 42—O my father, if this cup may not pass away from me except I drink it, thy will be done."

Here, again, Jesus is in fear of his life and wishes not to go through with the plans for his death.

I can well understand anyone dying being fearful, but what I don't understand is why Jesus is fearful of death when he has been told he will rise in three days. Jesus has been preaching that there is life after death in the kingdom of God and saying to all have faith, yet he has lost his. Could there be doubt in the mind of Jesus that his life would be restored?

I suspect there was doubt.

THE RESURRECTION

SAINT MATTHEW CHAPTER 28

VERSE 1—In the end of the Sabbath, as it began to dawn toward the first day of the week came Mary Magdalene and the other Mary to see the Sepulcher.

VERSE 2—And, behold, there was a great earthquake: for the angel of the Lord descended from heaven and came down and rolled back the stone from the door, and sat upon it.

VERSE 3—His countenance was like lightning and his raiment white as snow.

VERSE 4—And for fear of him the keepers did shake and became as dead men.

VERSE 5—And the angel answered and said unto the women, "Fear not ye, for I know that ye seek Jesus, which was crucified.

VERSE 6—He is not here; for he is risen." as he said, "Come, see the place there the Lord lay—

VERSE 7—And go quickly and tell his disciples that he is risen from the dead and behold he goeth before you into Galilee: there shall ye see him: Lo I have told you."

VERSE 8—And they departed quickly from the sepulcher with fear and great joy and did run to bring his disciples word.

VERSE 9—And as they went to tell his disciples, behold Jesus met them, saying all hail and they came and held him by the feet and worshipped him.

VERSE 10—Then said Jesus unto them, "Be not afraid to tell my brethren that they go into Galilee and there shall they see me."

VERSE 16—Then, the eleven disciples went away into Galilee into a mountain where Jesus had appointed them.

VERSE 17—And when they saw him, they worshiped him, but some doubted.

Here, in verse 17, it says, "But some doubted."

Let's look at Saint Luke chapter 24.

VERSE 15—And it came to pass that while they communed together and reasoned, Jesus himself drew near, and went with them.

VERSE 16—But their eyes were holden that they should not know him.

And in Saint Mark Chapter 16.

VERSE 12—After that, he appeared in another form unto two of them as they walked, and went into the country.

VERSE 13—And they went and told it unto the residue: neither believed they them.

VERSE 14—Afterward he (Jesus) appeared unto the eleven as they sat at meat and upbraided (reproached) them with their unbelief and hardness of heart because they believed not them which had seen him after he was risen.

Now, let's look at Saint John chapter 12.

VERSE 12—Mary is standing at the sepulchre door and seeth two angels in which sitting the one at the head and the other at the feet where the body of Jesus had lain.

VERSE 13—And they say unto her, "Woman why weepest thou?" She saith unto them, "Because they have taken away my Lord, and I know not where they have laid him."

VERSE 14—And when she had thus said, she turned herself back and saw Jesus standing and knew not that it was Jesus.

In these verses in the Bible, you will find that Jesus is not recognizable to anyone in the spirit or in the body form. So with this, I conclude that someone else is playing the final role for Jesus, and I believe Jesus's body was destroyed.

SUMMARY OF GOD 3:
JESUS CHRIST

THE CREATION of Jesus was the same as a test tube baby of today. God used the seed of David to fertilize Mary. David and Mary must have been of good genetic stature to produce a child of which God wanted his son by name only to look like.

God spent much time with Jesus, teaching him all that Jesus knew, for the people had problems understanding him for his intellect was so far above them. Also, you see where God introduces changes in his doctrines to Jesus, such as "an eye for an eye" is changed to "turn the other cheek." I feel Christ knew God as just a man with a lot of gadgetry to perform the feats that he did, and I believe this is why Jesus is finding it hard to give up his life.

Remember, God says Jesus would rise on the third day after his death, but by what means, spiritually or physically?

In St. John 20:30, Jesus is dying on the cross and said "It is finished," and he bowed his head and gave up the ghost. So this leaves us with the physical body that is going to be raised, but no one knew this body that Jesus claims to be in. This is why I feel someone else was playing out the final role.

If the events were as I have described, I feel Jesus is well justified in being remembered to have had the courage to give up his life for the reason of saving us from our sins.

The creation story may have sufficed 10,000 years ago. Out of cold, dark empty space God appears? And he said to the word, "say the word so creation can begin".

When I was about seventeen, my friend and I would sit in my car until 2 a.m. talking about religion and politics. I was always trying to figure out how the universe began and saying the word was my first clue, it was not who was the word, or what was the word; it was the vibration of the word. I worked on this theory for sixty years. It was 2012 when I felt I cracked the nut and wrote this book.

In this book you read that God says, "let us go down to Earth," and his angels would go down with him. This brings to my mind there is a big spaceship orbiting the earth and they were going up and down to this ship. And if an angel screwed up, he was stuck on the earth and not allowed back on the ship. God took no prisoners.

Moses talks to God as the burning bush. This bush is one of 1700 species of woody shrubs and trees. The burning bush leaves contain oils that when squeezed release a gas ignitable by a match.

Mary goes to the tomb where Jesus lay and the angels tell her, "He has gone, come and see." In other writing Mary is at the entrance of the tomb and she sees two angels inside, a bright light flashes, and the angels come out of the tomb and say, "Mary, he is not here." When Mary enters the tomb Jesus' body was gone. My theory is the angels, through some high-tech process, evaporated Jesus' body which left the image of his body on his burial cloth.

I have seen the burial cloth documentary showing the image of a body in 3-D imprinted on the cloth. Scientists don't know how this image was applied to the fabric. Tests show the cloth was made c. 1260-1390.

GOD 1
THE UNIVERSE

As I EXPLAINED in "God 3," I felt the Holy Ghost was God's way of explaining the physical laws of the universe.

In this chapter, I will try to explain how the laws of the universe work and how we respond to them.

When God said Adam and his descendants would become gods like them, he meant that we would follow in their footsteps.

This is to say, that through the process of evolution, we would develop to their level of intelligence.

Whatever solar system God and his angels came from, they also, at some time in their evolution, had to have believed in a god.

When a planet comes through evolution and it takes on an environment where it is possible for a life form such as us to develop, that life form will automatically look for a god to answer the question of "Where did I come from, and why?"

To fulfill this quest for a god, man invents gods such as the Egyptian gods: Ra, Horus, and Aten. The Greek God was Zeus. The Romans' was Jupiter. In India, a cow is worshipped, and so on.

When God and his angels came to earth, they knew that people needed a god to believe in, and so I believe they played out the role of a god.

This chapter is called "God 1: The Universe" because I believe the universe is the sole creator of life and all our actions are related to the laws of cause and effect.

ENERGY AND LIFE

Energy is the source of which we all need to sustain our existence, such as fuel for heat, food for our bodies, gas for our cars, and so on.

We are also energy. What life is, is a constant exchange of energy. For an example, the food we eat is changed into energy, which gives us life. Now that we have energy, we can build things that make energy, such as gasoline engines, which deliver energy. This energy can drive a generator, which makes electricity, which is also energy to light a bulb. The light can give energy to a plant to grow, and so on. So you can see how we live in a system that runs on energy exchange.

At the top of the list of sources of energy is the universe, for in its creation, the amount of energy was immeasurable. But all things in nature try to equalize, so all this energy has to be used up to become equal with its own self.

Let's use the big bang theory of the creation of the universe. We are actually living in the midst of a big explosion, which is of such magnitude we cannot see its ultimate results.

To try to explain this, let's say we take a firecracker and light it and throw it up into the air. Now, let's take a high-speed movie camera and film the explosion. Now let's rerun this film at normal speed, and what you will see is the debris of the firecracker spreading out from the center of the explosion.

Now, being in slow motion, this action is slowed down thousands of times, and we have the advantage to see each particle of debris as it leaves the center of the explosion until all the particles lose their outward motion and fall to the ground.

But the explosion of the universe is so immense and our life span so short we can see the total effect. What took place in seconds with the firecracker takes eons with the universe, and the debris of the universe are the stars and planets.

The energy of this explosion is being translated and transformed into other sources of energy, such as the outward motion of the stars and planets.

Heat and light from the stars are another form of transformation of this energy.

The effects of the light and heat on the planets are another form of energy transfer, which is where the energy of life comes from.

So the big bang is the main source of energy, and through cause and effect, this energy is translated into various other forms.

With the big bang being the primary source of creation and energy, the stars or suns are the secondary source, being that they are by-products then we are the by-products of our sun.

This is the start of energy exchange.

The sun is the main source of energy for the earth. Its energy is what causes our weather conditions, which in turn affects how plants, animals, and humans live.

Let's go back to the beginning of the earth where the primordial soup came into existence and started life at its lowest form, which was algae.

Through evolution, these algae had a mutation that was more complex and led to a higher life form, and this process went on and on until we have all the varieties of plants and animals we have today.

What you see happening is one form of life using another to sustain its life. The algae become food for a higher form of life, and that higher form of life becomes food for an even higher form of life, and so on.

What I'm trying to point out is that we are creatures of the universe and we conform to the laws of energy transfer. The sun was energy for the algae, so, in turn, the energy stored in the algae was the energy source of the next higher form, and so on.

We are also energy users, eating plants and animals, which are also energy from the sun, which is energy transformed.

Now that we have a chain of energy transfer, we can move on to the next step.

Everything that is alive has a predator that wants to use it for its energy value, so here is where self-defense comes in. Big fish eat smaller ones; animals eat other animals, us included. So here we have the law of survival of the fittest.

In nature, everything works by the law of least resistance, or the easiest way. Water will never go uphill because it's easier to go around it, and so it is with people. They also are looking for the easy way, and this is why people steal.

Let's take a caveman who just killed an animal for food, and another caveman comes along and sees the man with his fresh kill. He knows the trouble he had to get this animal, so he figures it is a lot easier to steal it than to hunt for another animal, so he subdues him and takes the kill.

Here is where good and evil and self-defense come into play.

Remember, we are still dealing with energy; that animal that was killed was energy.

As man develops, so does his method of transfer of energy. Now he is trading food for goods until we get up to today, where money is the common exchange of energy.

We exchange our energy at work for money. Money earned is in exchange for the energy we used working.

The money we earn buys food, which is energy again, so we have a complete cycle of energy exchange. Also involved with the exchange of energy is the problem of determining what's the fair exchange, which brought labor unions into existence. We get into competition, jealousy, and wars for energy. But what I want to point out is how it all got started and how our need for energy shapes our lives.

INTELLECT AND ITS ORIGIN

In the creation of the universe, I said we have energy and mass together as one, which represents nothing, and when the big bang occurred, they were separated and allowed for opposites, which are translated to us as hot and cold, light and dark, up and down, and so on.

When creation took place, we had the opposites, such as the heat of the explosion and the cold of empty space, the light from the blast and the dark that the light didn't reach.

And as the mass of the universe condensed, it also led to more and more opposites, so we have a foundation for opposites.

Here is where I feel the power to reason comes from, for we think in terms of yes and no; for example, your car is old and needs work done on it, so you ask yourself, "Should I spend money on it, or buy a new one?" If you decide to fix your car, you have said yes to that idea and have said no to the idea of buying a new one.

When you meet someone for the first time, you are deciding if you like them or not. The answer is either yes or no, and if you have no decision, then you are at the middle of yes and no, which stands for nothing. If you are not sure of your choice of either yes or no, then you are waxing and waning between the two.

In the beginning, life was at its most simple form. Its most important function was just being alive, not even being aware that it was.

Not until life forms became more complex, with nervous system for stimulation, did they do much of anything except eat. They must have had some sort of sensation that made them eat, just as we do when we are hungry.

So to stop the pain of hunger, we eat, and here is where I believe the learning process started. We learn through pain, and the opposite of pain is no pain.

A baby will stick its finger in a flame from lack of knowledge, but only once. The lesson was learned through pain.

When you were a child and did things wrong, Mom and Dad were there to give you a little pain.

As you get older, you learn to reason things out to get the best results out of a given situation, and what you are doing is choosing between the opposites.

LOVE AND EMOTION

The sun holds the planets in their orbits by an attraction called gravity; the planets are trying to get away through centrifugal force. But the orbits are not perfect; they wax and wane, speed up and slow down.

Just like the energy that holds their orbits, emotions of people work the same.

When a man and woman are attracted to each other, they go into orbit, or let's say, they go around with each other.

Just like the forces that hold the planets in orbit, the forces that hold the man and woman together are not perfect. They are waxing and waning, so in order to keep love alive between two people, they have to work at it by never getting too close or too far. For love is the fluxing of energy between the two.

If a planet gets too close to the sun, it will be pulled in, thus ends the energy of attraction. And the same applies to an overpowering person. Likewise, if a planet's outward force is too great, it will lose its attraction to the sun and get away, and also with people.

What I have tried to show here is how people relate to the laws of the universe; these are just the basic rules.

CIRCLES AND CYCLES

Everything in nature's construction is circular. At the very beginning of creation, the mass that exploded was circular, the pattern that the explosion made was circular, the planets and stars are circular, and so are their orbits.

In the world of microscopies, we have electrons, protons, neutrons, and quarks, which are all circular.

The basis for all substance is linked to a solar system where you have electrons orbiting a neutron or proton. So you can see we are pretty squared away on the round stuff.

Now that we have circular things with circular things going around them, this brings us into cycles.

Everything has cycles to it. The earth goes around the sun every 365 days, which is one cycle. The tides go in and out every six hours; that's a cycle. Then we have cycles with cycles. We are born, live, and die—that's one cycle. Our body cells are also having cycles just like us. They live and die, but they go through trillions of cycles to our one.

The weather and seasons have cycles, so everything has a beginning and an end, from the very small to the very large.

This also means that the universe will end when it completes its cycle, but since everything is round, that means there is no absolute end on the primary existence, which is the creation of the universe.

In the Bible, it says in the beginning there was nothing but black, empty space, and God was there with the word, which was with him as an entity separate from him. And God said to the word, "Say the word which will cause creation," and the word was spoken.

EVOLUTION

Things change through evolution. The planets and stars evolved from the universe; the earth is a product of that evolution. While the earth was forming, other elements of the earth were also going through the process of evolution. As the earth was condensing to a solid, gases were changed into air and water and forming other minerals, which came through the process of evolution. The earth was cooling down, forming ice caps on the poles; the seas were bringing life into existence. The life was going through evolutionary change also.

Evolution of one thing caused the evolution of another. As you read on from here, I will show how evolution leads to life after death.

GOVERNMENTS

Government is a law of nature and started millions of years ago in the formation of life.

It started when cells of an organism created a brain. The brain is a group of cells that responded to the environment around the body of cells, cells having a blueprint to follow from DNA organized and makes complex machines like ourselves for the sole purpose of security and an easier way of existing.

The reason our body was created was to have a mobile and a more efficient way of getting food. The brain is the government that makes decisions for the rest of the body. There is a rapport between the brain and the body. When there is trouble with the body, it sends a message to the brain. The brain then tries to solve the problem.

Our personalities are a by-product of this system, where the brain gets involved in other interests other than just the needs of the cells, which make up its body. When you look at lower forms of life, you can see that there is no personality. They relate only to what the brain was primarily designed to do, and that's to find food and protect the body. Look at a fish, give it a big smile. He won't smile back at you because it's too far down the scale of evolution.

Cells of the body are just like people of a civilization; they all have a specific job to do to maintain the system.

Let's take a person who drinks too much and causes an ulcer in his stomach. The doctor tells him to stop his drinking and go on a bland diet. The first knowledge of that ulcer was told to him by the cells in the stomach by giving him pain. But like the average person, he cheats on his diet to satisfy his taste for something spicy, being indifferent to the needs of the cells that are in distress.

So here is where you can see why the government of our country has a problem coming to the aid of its people. It's on its own pleasure trip and forgets its primary obligation.

LIFE AFTER DEATH

Through the process of evolution, I have tried to build a platform showing that the brain became somewhat divorced from the body by getting very involved with its environment.

This involvement with the environment led to who am I, what's it all about and who made me, which leads to the spirit or the invisible supreme being.

Here is where the brain is making its break with the physical body to relate to this spirit of creation. The brain or mind doesn't know for sure that there is a supreme being, but reasons that there is because of the lack of knowledge to explain where everything came from.

The brain, being alive with energy, now has a continuity with the universe, for the universe is full of energy of all kinds, such as radio waves, x-rays, gamma rays, light waves, magnetic waves, and waves of energy we've yet to discover. Here is where I believe the energy of the mind can get modulated with this energy of space and allow for such things as ESP and out-of-the-body ventures.

If my laws of evolution are correct about governments, then we have life after death.

This continuity between the brain and the universe completes the cycle of life and death, going back to the foundation of the universe being round, and therefore has no absolute end, then we have just gone full cycle.

Getting back to governments, let's look at the last law of a government, which is the fall of a government, where it has been defeated and the people are dying and deserted. What you see are the heads of government fleeing, for they do not die with their people.

And this is the reason why I believe our personalities do not die with our bodies; their escape route is into the next dimension, which is energy. This will also bring us full cycle for our energy source.

What is it like to be alive in the dimension energy? My guess would be it has its problems there, just as we have here.

On earth we have physical pain; on the other side, I would venture to say the problems are emotional, which would explain a ghost who haunts where he lived physically.

There could also be a process of evolution in that dimension as there is on earth. I felt God 2 has control of this dimension. As I said, they made a scientific breakthrough and conquered the universal energy. This is to say there is probably an established government on the other side.

In this book that we are clones, so this also makes us their property to do with us as they will.

So I will end by saying, you better be good.

Besides, I feel man doesn't have the intelligence to keep the problems of earth in order; we need a government of the world and run by someone more intelligent than us.

I do feel God is coming back and soon. There will be those who will resist. These are the ones who are leaders now but will have to submit their powers for the change of command, and the earth will be a better place for you and me.

GOD 1:
THE UNIVERSE
LIFE: THE STRAIGHT
AND NARROW ROAD

IN MY THEORY of the universe being God 1 the creator of all things, you can see how, by the law of opposites, life, the straight and narrow road as Jesus said, fits in. If we judge everything by its opposite, then the center is nothing. For example, take a straight line and we'll call it the center line of opposites. It also represents nothing, and it can be called the narrow road of life.

Let me try to explain by using lines to show the opposites.

0 ————————————————————

This line represents zero; it's the state of the universe before the big bang. This line also represents perfection. I coined it ZIP, meaning zero is perfection.

As I have said earlier, the universe was perfect until the big bang. To be absolutely perfect, there is no need for anything. This would have to be a temporary state; since everything is circular, this point of perfection would be the beginning of the universe and the end.

After the big bang, the line looks like this.

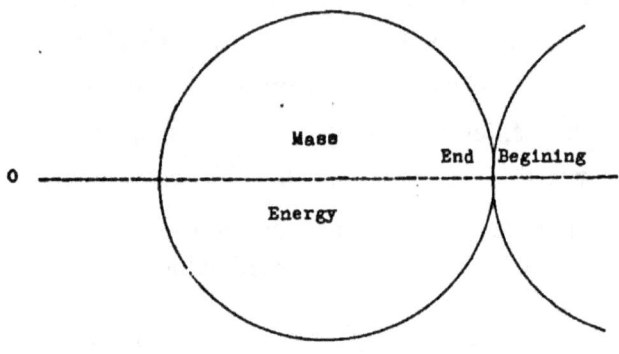

Mass and energy are now separated, which is the beginning of opposites. As Jesus said, the road of life is straight and narrow. The zero line runs down the center of the road of life. This line represents zero and perfection.

You can't make any gain if you stay dead center on this line. So you have to deviate on either side of this line or road, and the opposites are on either side of this road or line. I see the road of life as a tight rope. As a high-wire walker in a circus walks on the high wire, he is balancing on the wire, which is swaying back and forth, while he tries to keep his balance.

Let's look at this high wire as our zero line. In order for the wire walker to get to the other side, he has to disturb the perfect state of the wire. As he works on keeping his balance, his swaying back and forth is his opposites, which he is working with; if he gets too far away from the straight and narrow, he will fall.

And so it is with our everyday life. We cannot get too far from the center line or we get into trouble. This is how the line works for us.

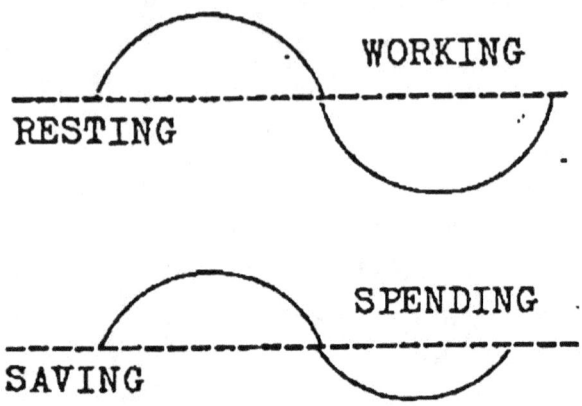

These are just two examples of how we have to walk the straight and narrow, by balancing between all of two opposites.

In our lives we have a formula for everything that has to do with technology. If you want to know what size of heating system to put in your house, there is a formula to tell you.

If you want to know how much fuel it would take to send a rocket to Mars, there is a formula for it. But for the basic problems of everyday life, we have no formula.

I feel the basic rule or foundation would be the law of cause and effect, the law of nature, and another law would be, for every action there is an equal and opposite reaction .We have heard this law as "An eye for an eye and a tooth for a tooth" but was later changed to "Turn the other cheek."

I feel that by using these laws, we could have a better system of justice.

For example, if a person steals your car and destroys it, instead of locking him up and paying taxes to clothe and feed him, put him to work to pay back the value of that car he stole and the cost of your inconvenience. By this system, you would be using a law of nature. Every action has an equal and opposite reaction. Our system can never be perfect, for perfection is that zero line.

SUMMARY OF GOD 1

IF WE ARE a product or creation of a supreme being, then one would think we would inherit his righteousness. But we didn't; this is to say we are the crows out of a dove's nest.

If we are a product or creation of the universe, then I feel we inherited all its ills of imperfection.

When Adam and Eve were in the Garden of Eden, they had no worries. For God was tending to all their needs. But this had to end because this situation had God as the servant. So in order to turn the situation around, God came up with the forbidden fruit tree. Let's say if Adam and Eve never broke the rules and neither did all their descendants, then God would become a slave to us in order to maintain a paradise.

People go through life wondering what it is all about and what the purpose of life is. I feel that there is no purpose to life.

What is life? It's what you make of it.

Life is motion. If something doesn't move, we say it is lifeless.

SUMMARY OF GOD 1

WHO AM I? What should I do with my life? Why am I doing what I am doing? Should I be doing what I am doing? These questions come about because our personalities are by-products of what the brain's primary function was. And that was eating and self-defense.

Here is where I feel people should be educated to the fact that there is no purpose to life, so they will not waste their time looking for one. Let me use my theory of opposites to show my point. The universe is in motion, so we can say it has life, but before the big bang, it had no motion, so it also had no life.

And for the same reason that it is moving or has life is the same as us having life, which is no reason. It's just a case of cause and effect. What is important in life? Nothing.

There is nothing that has any importance or value; these are all man-made ideas of value and priorities, which come about through the choices of opposites. Here again is my zero line, representing nothing as the foundation of everything.

I find people are always looking for someone to solve their problems for them. Whoever they choose will always let them down, for it's an illusion. I have a saying that I feel explains the situation, which is "Everyone is looking for a mother."

When we were children, it was our mother who solved all our problems, but as we got older, we found that our mother couldn't solve our adult problems and was having trouble with her own.

So this situation leads us to look for someone who can fill Mother's role, which leads us to governments and the Supreme Being.

As God said, "I am Lord thy God, and put no other Gods before me," he also said we were made in his image, so this tells me that I am also a god and should not put another man before me. If you allow a man to be above you, he will accept this position and act accordingly, and by the same token, if you take the position that he is no better than you as a man, he will also accept this, for he knows this to be true.

If the sun said to the earth, "I am better than you because I shine and give you light and energy to prosper," then the earth would say, "Be thankful for me, for without me, you would be alone in the dark and there would be no one to need you, and you would be useless."

SUMMARY OF GOD 1

THIS IS TO SAY we all have our own thing to do, and whatever it is, we still need each other. If you use the human body for an example, you can see who, why, and what we are as a civilization. Consider yourself as a cell in a living body. You would have a specific job to do. Let's say you are a cell in the heart. As a cell in the heart, you are only one of many thousands just like you, which doesn't make your existence very important. If you die, there is no great loss. You will be replaced, and it's the same with whatever job you are doing as a person.

The important thing is to keep the system going. All forms of life have a system, and all for the same reason, and that is to get energy the easiest way. As a cell all alone, your life would be very uncertain, but if you joined a group and developed a system, your odds of survival would go up, and you would be sure of your share of energy for doing your part in the system.

Your body is such a system. Its main function is keeping all its cells alive. This system does not cater to the individual, only the mass as a whole.

Arteries in the body are like highways across the land, carrying food for energy to all the cells. The nervous system in the body carries information to the brain, just as telephone wires carry information to the government.

Everything we do as a people is a copy of nature. We build machines to do work for us; the cells in our bodies built us as their machine to work for them.

The machines we build break down, and we repair them just like the cells that repair our bodies. The country has an electrical system that powers it; so does our bodies.

The states have police to ensure the common good; the body has white blood cells to arrest the troublemakers. The country has an army to defend it; the body is itself the army of cells, which will fight to protect itself. Through the command of its government or brain, all higher life forms have some sort of defense system.

These are the reasons why we as people unit together to form a system to ensure our safety and form a government to be the control center, or as in the body, the brain.

So I think you can see the similarities. But as I said before, our personalities are by-products of our minds and got divorced from its basic function, which was to feed and protect its body.

And I believe it's the same with our government. It also forgot its primary function, and by my theory, you can understand how and why.

What I'm trying to point out is that our personalities are a separate entity, which evolved out of a system whose primary function was eating and self-defense.

Now that we live in a system that insures food and protection, we can spend great amounts of time dealing with our personalities, and here is where the plot thickens.

What is personality?

It's a cause-and-effect reaction based on how you interpret your environment, the kind of environment you're in, and how you choose your values, also how you feel physically and your attitude about yourself. Now this is your mental personality.

Your body also has a personality, which is how tall, how big, how strong, the color of eyes, hair, and so on, which is also a cause-and-effect reaction based on the chemistry of the body.

Likewise, the country we live in has a personality, which comes about through its government, which is the mind or brain of the body of people who live in it.

Let's make a comparison. Imagine the cells in your body as little people and your mind as the government of these people. Say, you want to get drunk, and knowing you will be sick, you do it anyway. The little people or cells in your body are protesting the decision you made by making you sick. And when the government of a country overindulges in something that is bad for its people, like nuclear reactors, the people also protest to upset the government on its bad decision, which falls under the law of cause and effect.

Now let's go back to energy. I had said earlier that energy is the fuel that runs everything and that we are a product of this energy and are energy ourselves.

Remember, I said the body is a machine and a civilization of cells whose sole function is to get energy the easiest and safest way, and our personalities are by-products of this system, which came through evolution.

Likewise, our personalities are looking for energy. Since the personality came through evolution, the energy source it's looking for also came through evolution with the personality.

Let's look back at the caveman. All that we have today is just what he didn't have.

His biggest problem was staying alive, so his time was devoted to eating and protecting himself.

If you were to put this caveman on our welfare system today, he would think he died and went to heaven.

Because this would solve all his problems, for his personality hasn't acquired a hunger for the energy of the mind.

What is the energy of the mind?

Stimulation. We need things to stimulate our minds or we get bored.

We are also looking for security and the easy way of life.

Today, we have all kinds of things to stimulate us, such as radio, TV, sports, movies, cars, boats, and so on. Now to get all these things, we need money. Money is energy in its evolutes form. We lie, cheat, steal, and in some cases, kill for money (energy).

COMPETITION

Man competes with man for everything; he competes for a job, a woman, even to be the first one away at a green light. Man's games are also competitive. I feel this competition came about through the law of the survival of the fittest. Since this law is millions of years old, it has a deep root in our personalities.

The system of government we live in runs by competition. Our religious system runs on moral values, which are to keep our everyday competition free of lying, cheating, stealing, and so on. If we didn't have moral values, the system of competition would self-destruct.

ENERGY

Since people are energy, they are also used for their energy value; it started with slavery. But as the moral values of man went up, they came in conflict with slavery. But people are still used today for their energy value, only in a more subtle way. As I have said before, the little fish is food (energy) for the bigger fish, and the bigger fish is food (energy) for an even bigger fish.

This process of energy exchange goes on in all forms of life. All life forms have a predator, and man also has a predator, and it's his fellow man that seeks him for his energy value, which is money.

How your predator gets you is through confidence.

Radio and TV commercials give you confidence that whatever they are selling is the best. Politicians give us confidence that they will correct the system.

The car salesman gives us confidence that

the car we are buying is a cream puff. Our children give us confidence by saying they will be home early and won't hot-rod the car. So you can see people will say or do anything to get what they want out of you, and what they want is one or more of three things: money (energy), security, and stimulation.

What I have tried to show is that the foundation of life and society is energy and the law of cause and effect.

So for these reasons, I believe we came through an evolutionary process, and God, being of greater intelligence and farther along in evolution, helped us in the transition to modern man with moral values.

As it looks to me, it all began this way. In the beginning there was nothing, not even a beginning.

Empty space is nothing, so how can nothing have a beginning? And if it has no beginning, it cannot have an ending. What we have now is eternity. Space has no beginning and no end; it's forever.

Space is emptiness of any matter, any light, and any temperature. It would be at point zero, where, if there were molecules in space, they could not move. At this point, I am telling my story when space was totally empty.

What I want to say is how all we know of space and the planets was created from nothing.

The main ingredients of the universe are motion and energy. Motion can create energy, and energy can create motion. Neither has any substance. What I am getting to is to say that the universe was made from nothing.

The very first particle was made from nothing. It was made from motion. Motion and energy have no substance. In order to get motion, we need energy.

We need energy to make a particle from nothing. So how can we create energy from empty space? We need motion. You see, we need energy to make motion and motion to make a particle.

Space is endless, and at a temperature not conducive for motion. So the first thing we need is to get the temperature of space up. This is how it was done. Space, being so large, created a temperature differential within its self, causing a rise in temperature for motion.

The motion from the increase in temperature created motion, which created a distortion of space in the form of waves. It would look like the heat waves coming off a hot road in the summer. Now we have a vibration.

Imagine an asphalt road running as far as you can see with heat waves rising from it, and on both sides of this road, the temperature is 400 degrees below zero. These heat waves are rising from the road and being pushed to the sides of the road where they are instantly frozen.

Those heat waves are being frozen while they are still in motion. What we have is energy frozen in motion. It is like a mouse trap ready to go off, but it can't until the temperature is above freezing again.

At this point, we have a distortion of space in the shape of a wave that would be a vibration. The area of space this action is taking place would be measured in light-years. As these waves of vibrations are moving, they are also being pushed into the 400-below zero area of space where they are instantly frozen.

We do not have a particle yet. We have motion locked up, and this is now energy locked up. We can call this dark matter and dark energy.

This is coagulating into a massive diameter in light-years in size, and at a critical time, this mass has gravity pulling it to a density that is generating heat and is allowing this mass of frozen energy to explode, and it is known as the big bang that created a massive sun. This is how matter was created from nothing. This is why nothing matters in our lives, because nothing is the foundation of everything.

Roy Manish
3-15-14

MY THEORY OF
THE CREATION OF
THE UNIVERSE

BY ROY MANISH

I HAVE PONDERED the creation or the beginning of space and matter a long time and religious stories of how it all began.

I always thought space should not exist if we are talking about nothing in the beginning. If we have space then space is something.

Now we are talking about endless space, not only endless but empty space. However here we are, literally made from nothing. But it took billions of years for us to arrive. What I want to talk about is the nothingness of space.

Think about this, as far as your mind can imagine how big space is, what could be in it and coagulate to cause a reaction to cause creation.

Energy is the main factor, it was energy that caused the so called big bang.

But what caused the energy?

There had to be something in space reacting with something else to cause a reaction that gave off enormous energy to start the big bang.

It would be like lighting a match in a gas-filled room.

Let's take a different point of view, let's imagine there was no space in the beginning and the expansion of energy created space. But this brings us back to what caused the energy.

So let's work with endless empty space but first I believe the answers are in our midst we and all of nature respond to the energy of creation.

Before the big bang the temperature was absolute zero -459.67 degrees Fahrenheit or maybe not!

If there were particles in space at zero temperature, there could not be any movement of any kind. If there was no movement nothing could happen. But something did happen, this means the temperature had to rise or it was never absolute zero.

So what caused the temperature to rise? Here is where dark matter and dark energy. Come into the picture.

Dark energy is where we should begin because this is where the universe came from.

The universe was the size of a baseball before the Big Bang.

If in the beginning the universe was the size of a baseball, to me this a big clue. If all the planets and suns came from this ball we are talking a huge amount of compressed energy, at this point you have to think big and I mean real big.

When we are talking the size of a baseball we mean this baseball is the end of the collapsing of a much bigger sphere, and it's this sphere is where you have to think big. Think light years.

Think how planets are made, one grain

of sand will collect another grain, two grans will have more attraction and collect more and so one and over time you have a planet. This is what I think happened with the + and - Charge of empty space. Think about an idea you have and where did it come from and what is it made of?

I am inclined to believe that there is a frequency or a vibration to all matter, for example sound, light, heat, your heart beat, radio/TV and all the music we hear are all frequencies. So this leads me to believe that the very beginning there was nothing in space, but the energy of just being space. And maybe there was a frequency in space. I remember it was said that in the beginning there was nothing but God and the entity and God said to the entity, say the word so creation can begin and the word was spoken. Whatever the word was it had a frequency, and there is no evidence of a word hanging around in space. But in the string theory there is a frequency of motion of matter going in and out of existence.

But we are talking about matter, that we don't know if it exists, so I am going to sum up my theory. We have space that, as far as we know, the temperature is at absolute zero and as far as we know, no particles of matter can move at absolute zero. Then the temperature must have risen to allow for motion. What caused the temperature to rise?

Or it was never at absolute zero, and cannot become absolute zero. Next, there had to be particles of opposite charges to unite and repel. Unlike charges would cancel themselves out. The like particles would have survived by just chance.

Now, the gravity of each particle of the same charge are gathering together to make a ball that is invisible. As this ball is getting bigger and bigger, the unlike charges coming in contact with this ball are annihilated. This annihilation would cause a rise in temperature, making movement for like and unlike particles faster.

The warmer space got, the more annihilation was happening. At the same time, another ball could be in the making of the opposite charge. However, it would have to be a great distance from our first ball, or the annihilation of both would end any progress.

Where I am going here is that two spheres could be in progress, but light years apart from each other. Over time, they would be getting bigger and bigger independently of each other.

At the same time, annihilation would be going on throughout space.

In the meantime, our two spheres of different charges would be getting bigger and bigger, and at some point in unknown time they would come together and cause the unleashing of energy that we call The Big Bang Theory.

My other theory would be that only one sphere survived and was so large in size, gravity pulled in so densely that it became a star that went supernova.

This star could shine for billions years before it went nova, which would leave us with a black hole at the Beginning. The universe is expanding because there was density to space. When the big bang took off, it pushed space away to make way for the heat and newly created matter compressing space. Now space is decompressing and pushing the galaxies away.

Dark matter is the other sphere that did not get large enough to ignite, but has a gravitational field. I have to go with the idea space is, was, and always was here.

It's not a thing, it's a void (emptiness); but we need a comparison to something! If I draw a box on a sheet of paper, I can say the box is empty. But if I erase the box, then I say the paper is empty, so where does it end?

It's hard to come to grips with something that has no boundaries. As far as we know, we have to think outside the box.

I like the string theory where matter is popping in and out of existence. And at some point it stayed in existence. This popping in and out is the cause of a vibration—or the vibration caused the popping in and out. This is where you say, what came first the chicken or the egg? I'm going with the chicken. And I am going with the vibration was first.

I like to look at the same laws of physics we understand, and apply them to the universe. The earth was formed by particles of matter that gravity compressed together. The gravity of particles in space did the same thing only on a much grander scale.

Just as the particle made the earth, the gravity pulled these particles in so tight that it created heat, and the heat caused eruptions, earthquakes, and volcanoes.

In empty space, the same process could be what started the universe; but it went way beyond making a planet, to making a huge star. This could be one of countless stars that lit and heated space. The explosion in the process caused a vibration, making more particles to pop into matter. These suns were so massive when they went nova that they gave off all the matter that created the planets, and died as black holes—which explains why all galaxies have black holes in their centers.

My theory of how it all began is this. In the beginning there was nothing, not even a beginning. Empty space is nothing. So how can nothing have a beginning? And if it has no beginning, it cannot have an ending.

What we have now is eternity; space is forever. Space is emptiness of any matter, and it's pitch black. It would be at point zero, where if there were molecules in space they could not move.

My theory is that space was totally empty.

The main ingredient of the universe is motion, and energy motion can create energy, and energy can create motion. Neither has any substance.

The very first particle was made from nothing. It was made from motion. In order to get motion, we need energy. So how can we create energy from empty space? We need motion. We need energy to make motion, and motion to make a particle.

Space is at a temperature not conducive for motion. We need to get the temperature of space up. This is how it was done; space being so large created a temperature differential within itself, causing a rise in temperature for motion.

The motion from the increase in temperature created motion, which created a distortion of space in the form of waves. It would look like the heat waves coming off a hot road in the summer. Now we have a vibration.

Imagine an asphalt road running as far as you can see with heat waves rising from it and on both sides of this road the temperature is 400 degrees below zero.

These heat waves are rising from the road and being pushed to the sides of the road, where they are instantly frozen.

Those heat waves are being frozen while they are still in motion. What we have is energy frozen in motion. It is like a mouse trap ready to go off, but it can't until the temperature is above freezing again.

At this point we have a distortion of space in the shape of waves that would be a vibration. The area of space where this action took place would be measured in light years. As these waves of vibrations are moving, they are also being pushed into the 400 degrees below zero area of space, where they are instantly frozen.

We do not have a particle yet. We have motion locked up, and this is now energy locked up. We can call this dark matter and dark energy.

This is coagulating into a massive diameter light years in size, and at a critical time, this mass has gravity, pulling this mass to a density that is generating heat and is allowing this mass of frozen energy to explode. This is known as The Big Bang that created a massive sun. The creation of suns is where particles are created from fusion. This is how matter was created from nothing.

Roy Manish
3-15-14

SECRET OF LIFE

Through the years I have heard, What's the secret of life? What is the point of being alive?

We are here for a short time. We gain knowledge and wisdom, then we die.

Right now we are a very high-tech society and we rely on this technology for our survival. If tomorrow we wake up and this technology is gone, we will be back to the Stone Age, and millions of us will starve to death.

We will be the only animal that will miss this lifestyle. But not the lions, tigers and bears, and the fishes in the deep blue sea.

So this brings us to the fact our life hinges on survival. Are we alive just to survive day by day? So, what is the secret of life? The secret is one word. The word is *motion*.

Think about what you do all the time. It's moving—we are always moving. And when you stop moving, you are dead. So the secret of life is motion. Your life is based on how you move with it. You've heard people say, "What are you going to do with your life? Are you moving in the right direction?"

You may want to be the president of the United States, so you move to become the president by learning law and running for political office of some kind to gain knowledge. This is how you direct your motion.

Life is just motion. The whole universe is in motion, and it moves with no intent, but because we have a brain, we move with intent

The other part of the secret are the words *nothing* and *energy*.

We have energy to power our motion, and the reason for our life is nothing or no reason. The universe was created from nothing, so there is no foundation that it's built on. This means there are no rules, so anything goes.

RAM
1-29-16

THE SECRET PART 2

WE HUMANS DEAL with things in life that do not exist. We live in a virtual reality world. This doesn't mean the world is not real and all the things we touch are not real.

We live in our minds and are trapped in a real physical body. What is real you can put in a bucket.

Here are the things you can't put in a bucket: words, ideas, motion, feelings, smell, taste, love, hate, joy, fun, drama, beliefs, hope, fear, sorrow, stress, tiredness, excitement, sexual attraction, pain, the feeling of touch, the feeling of temperature, the images of what you see, depression, desire, wanting, missing, and life.

This is the world we live in, and it's not real. Not one of the words in that list can you hold in your hand. We are trapped in a physical body and live in a physical universe. You can feel very much alive, but if the body dies, you die with it.

Your brain is a physical thing, but you are not; you are the energy the brain creates. Think of it like the northern lights, the Aurora Borealis. The energy your brain creates is like the northern lights, and that light is you.

RAM

THE NEAR END OF HUMANS

THE HUMAN RACE will evolve into a mechanical machine to end death and disease, and will be at war with those who are of flesh.

The new mechanical race will be programmed to fit wherever the government needs them. Humans need years of education, whereas the mechanical man can download in minutes in any profession needed. Doctors will be electronic technicians/programmers.

The mechanical men will have no free will. The very rich will remain human, so as not to give up the desires of the flesh, and have control over the mechanical man.

The very rich will be able to download their personality into human replacement bodies to avoid death. Their identity will also be saved on a chip for backup.

There will be genocide of the world's population. The mechanical men will be the space men of the future.

The planets that humans want to go to that are like earth are hundreds of light-years away. Only the mechanical man can make such a journey that is far away.

The seeds of the human will go to these great distances with the mechanical man to regenerate the human race on the new planets.

I think, using ink jet printer technology, a human could be printed in 3-D using all the different body cells. In hours or even less, a full-size human could be created. This is probably how we arrived here on earth thousands of years ago.

It's doubtful the Adam and Eve story will exist on the new worlds. If you are not rich and human, you won't have a prayer to survive. Morality will not exist.

When the time comes that everything is manufactured by a robot and computer-operated machinery, there will be no need for a human. It will be like turning the clock back to the days of plantation owners when they had slaves. But now they will have robots working for them. They could go to the Internet and order the right robot to fill their needs.

Driverless cars delivering your food. Drones flying around your property, monitoring the peasants that want to kill you. These are the people that killed the humans to gain a country. Now they own the world and have their sights on planets.

If they find a planet they want that has low-IQ humans on it, they will tell them they are gods and created the universe.

Does this story have a ring to it?

RAM

ABOUT THE AUTHOR

Born in Warwick, Rhode Island, in 1939 of working-class parents, Roy, at eleven years old, was setting up duck pins in a bowling alley. At twelve, he drove family cars and made friends with three factory watchmen, and he drove a forklift for fun. He left school at sixteen to work in a jewelry shop as a solderer. At age sixteen, he enrolled at New England Tech for radio and TV repair and worked as an auto mechanic. At twenty he worked at Fruit of the Loom, dying cloth. At twenty-six he worked at Electric Boat as an electrician. And at twenty-seven, he worked at a cup factory as a lead man and foreman and machine designer. He married at twenty-six and had one child, and he retired at sixty-one.

His interest was always about everything in the world of space and science. He had a hard time believing in God. When he was sixteen, in bed one night, he said to God, "If you really exist, I want you to prove it to me. I want you to tell me my future," and about a year later, I did see my future. I can say with no doubt he does exist.

The Soul of

The Prophet's

Health

Ken Cox

REJOICE
Essential Publishing

Ken Cox/Rejoice Essential Publishing
PO BOX 512
Effingham, SC 29541
www.republishing.org

Unless otherwise indicated, scripture is taken from the King James Version.'

The Soul of The Prophet's Health/Ken Cox